Discover:

The Ethical Frontier of Artificial Intelligence

A Guide to Navigating the Impact of AI
on Work, Workers, and Society

By Brendan T. Reilly

ISBN: 9798877362017

When it comes to Artificial Intelligence "I'm increasingly inclined to think there should be some regulatory oversight, maybe at the national and international level just to make sure that we don't do something very foolish." – Elon Musk

Table of Contents

ACKNOWLEDGMENTS

I extend my deepest gratitude to the researchers, scientists, and AI experts whose pioneering work in AI has been the foundation and inspiration for this book. Special thanks to the AI Ethics Boards and Council Members at AIworkforce.org for their vital insights on AI's ethical implications, ensuring technology aligns with human values. My family and friends deserve immense appreciation for their unwavering support throughout this journey. Lastly, I thank you, the readers, for your keen interest in exploring AI's complexities and its societal impact. Your engagement is pivotal in shaping a future where AI benefits human life while upholding our values. This book is a collaborative effort, and I am profoundly thankful for everyone's contributions to this enlightening exploration of AI and ethics.

PREFACE

The Paradox of Progress: A Prelude to the AI Era

The dawn of the AI era marks a turning point in human history, characterized by rapid technological advancements and transformative changes. Artificial Intelligence stands as both a symbol of progress and a catalyst for disruptive changes across various sectors. "AI Ethics - A Guide to Navigating the Ethical Frontier of Artificial Intelligence" embarks on an exploration of AI's dual nature - as a driver of innovation and as a significant disruptor of jobs, industries, and societal norms. This book aims to unravel the intricate narrative of AI's influence, offering insights into its profound implications on the global workforce, the economy, and society. This Preface sets the context for the discussions that follow, painting a picture of the current landscape of AI development and its multifaceted impacts. It prepares readers for a journey through the complex world of AI, setting the stage for a deep dive into the ethical, societal, and economic challenges and opportunities presented by this groundbreaking technology.

The Alarming Forecast – A World Transformed by AI

In the initial part of this book, we examine a series of disconcerting reports and forecasts from authoritative sources like Bloomberg, Forbes, BBC as well as industry leaders PwC, Goldman Sachs, and McKinsey & Company. The forecasts from these organizations depict a dire picture of the global workforce's future under the influence of rapidly progressing Artificial Intelligence. McKinsey's analysis on the impact of AI from December 2023 stands out, predicting that over 300 million jobs could be rendered obsolete globally within the next decade due to AI, potentially impacting nearly a billion people. This daunting forecast was echoed by PwC and Goldman Sachs in early 2024, each projecting a similar magnitude of job losses attributable to AI.

These statistics go beyond mere numerical predictions; they illustrate the deep impact on individuals, families, and communities worldwide. This book aims to delve into these significant shifts, exploring the expansive implications of AI-induced job displacement, which span industries and even global communities. In this book we also look at the benefits of Artificial Intelligence from its ability to enhance medical research and clean energy solutions to its ability to simplify day-to-day work and life tasks.

A Dual-Edged Sword: Job Creation and Displacement by AI

The narrative throughout this book probes into a more optimistic short-term forecast from the New York Times and Forbes, that suggest that AI could create 97 million new jobs over the next decade. These jobs represent significant opportunities for many around the world. However, the book also critically examines the long-term challenges of continued enhancements of AI.

While AI's potential to create millions of new jobs in the upcoming decade is often highlighted, there remains a pervasive skepticism. Many believe that a significant fraction of these new roles, born from AI's progress and increased accessibility, may themselves be susceptible to future automation by the same technology. This concern is exacerbated by the current lack of robust regulatory frameworks and ethical guidelines for AI deployment. Such a conundrum underscores the pressing necessity for thorough AI oversight that marries legislative initiatives with ethical deliberations to guide the responsible integration of AI into society.

The Future in an AI-driven World

"AI Ethics - A Guide to Navigating the Ethical Frontier of AI" meticulously examines the extensive reach of AI's influence, underscoring the vital role of guidance, oversight, and regulation. It emphasizes striking a crucial balance - harnessing AI for its potential in driving job growth and enhancing sectors like marketing, retail, healthcare, research, and manufacturing, while being acutely aware of the possible widespread job disruptions it might cause in the future.

This book delves into the disproportionate impact of AI across various sectors, offering insights into the specific challenges that certain job categories, industries, regions, and countries might encounter. It highlights the need for fairness and equity in a transformative job market reshaped by AI.

The narrative also tackles the societal, ethical, and regulatory complexities introduced by AI. It argues for strategic and equitable approaches that integrate technological innovation with adherence to ethical standards and societal welfare. The book presents a balanced view, contemplating AI's potential to transform industries and improve efficiency, alongside the significant human implications, such as employment shifts, the evolving nature of work, and broader societal repercussions.

Balancing the Equation: AI's Benefits and Job Losses

As the book navigates the complex transition in the workforce brought about by AI advancements, it advocates for a multi-faceted approach to the ethical deployment of AI. This includes encouraging industries to prepare for changes, urging governments to create supportive policies and safety nets, and emphasizing the role of education in preparing future generations for an AI-dominated world.

The analysis extends beyond the job market, examining AI's broader societal implications. It discusses AI's potential contributions to solving complex global challenges, like climate change and healthcare crises, and the possibility of exacerbating issues such as inequality and ethical dilemmas which if not properly managed could lead to social and political unrest and even conflict.

The Ethical Imperative in AI Development

In the latter part of "AI Ethics - A Guide to Navigating the Ethical Frontier of AI", the focus shifts to exploring perceptions of AI's risks from leading figures in the AI sphere. The book delves deeply into Elon Musk's alarming depiction of AI as "the most disruptive force in history," as discussed in his November 2023 conversation with the UK Prime Minister Rishi Sunak. Musk's stark warnings about AI's potential to threaten humanity are thoroughly analyzed, providing a nuanced understanding of his concerns regarding the ethical, social, and economic fallout from uncontrolled AI advancement.

Further, the book taps into the insightful dialogue between Bill Gates and OpenAI's CEO Sam Altman. Their discussion, broadcast on Gates' podcast in January 2024, sheds light on Altman's proposition for a global regulatory body for AI, drawing parallels to the International Atomic Energy Agency's role in nuclear oversight. Altman envisions this body functioning akin to weapons inspectors, critically evaluating the capabilities of significant AI infrastructures globally. This recommendation, stemming from Altman's interview, underscores AI's potential geopolitical ramifications and underscores the necessity for a cohesive, global regulatory approach.

The second half of the book rigorously investigates principles of fairness, transparency, and accountability in AI development, dissecting legislative frameworks in the United States and Europe. It critically assesses the sufficiency of existing laws and the imperative for new regulations tailored to AI's unique challenges. The discourse then broadens to underscore the need for an international ethical framework for AI, advocating for global cooperation and standard-setting to keep pace with AI's rapid evolution.

Building on Altman's suggestions, the book explores the conceivable structure and operational dynamics of a global AI regulatory body, addressing potential challenges such as innovation impediment, equitable AI access, and balancing national interests with global collaboration.

Furthermore, the book provides a global perspective on AI's impact on job markets, examining how AI reshapes industries and professions, from architecture and law to software development and truck driving. It scrutinizes the nature of job displacement, the evolving value of human labor, and the ethical ramifications of AI in a workforce increasingly dominated by automation.

In its concluding chapters, the book addresses the ongoing AI Arms Race, triggered by the Biden Administration's October 2022 decision to restrict advanced microchip technology sales to China. It delves into the geopolitical complexities surrounding Taiwan's independence and its central role in the global chip manufacturing industry.

The book culminates by urging readers to reflect on AI's immense potential and its capacity to both foster unprecedented advancements and disrupt established job markets. It highlights the ethical urgency for a thoughtful approach to AI's development and deployment, acknowledging the profound societal and employment implications of AI's unchecked progress.

In summary, "AI Ethics - A Guide to Navigating the Ethical Frontier of AI" is a comprehensive exploration of the multifaceted impact of AI, emphasizing the need for a global, ethically-informed strategy to harness AI's benefits while mitigating its potential for societal disruption.

"The pace of progress in artificial intelligence (I'm not referring to narrow AI) is incredibly fast. Unless you have direct exposure to groups like Deepmind, you have no idea how fast—it is growing at a pace close to exponential. The risk of something seriously dangerous happening is in the five-year time frame. 10 years at most."

– Elon Musk

Chapter 1: The Evolution of AI: From Concept to Core Technology

Artificial Intelligence (AI) has undergone a dramatic evolution, transforming from a theoretical concept in the mid-20th century to a core technology reshaping various aspects of our world. Initially, AI was about imitating human intelligence through rule-based systems. However, the advent of machine learning and deep learning marked a paradigm shift, enabling AI to learn and adapt from data rather than follow pre-programmed rules.

Recent Advancements in AI Technology

The advancements in Artificial Intelligence (AI) are deeply intertwined with the evolution of computing infrastructure and chip technology. One of the key drivers of AI's progress has been the significant enhancements in cloud computing capabilities. Cloud platforms offer scalable and flexible computing resources, crucial for AI algorithms that require substantial computational power. This scalability is vital for processing large datasets and executing complex AI models, particularly in fields like deep learning.

In tandem with cloud computing, the development of GPU (Graphics Processing Unit) technology has been fundamental to AI's growth. Originally designed for rendering graphics in video games, GPUs have proven highly efficient for parallel processing tasks essential in AI computations. Their ability to handle multiple operations simultaneously makes them ideal for the matrix and vector computations used in machine learning and deep learning algorithms.

Additionally, the advent of specialized AI chips has further accelerated AI development. These chips are specifically designed to optimize the performance of AI algorithms, enhancing their efficiency in data processing tasks. Unlike general-purpose processors, AI chips are tailored to handle the unique requirements of AI computations, such as tensor operations in neural networks. This specialization not only speeds up AI processing but also reduces energy consumption, contributing to more sustainable AI operations.

This technological evolution, encompassing cloud computing, GPUs, and specialized AI chips, has significantly expanded AI's potential applications. From healthcare to autonomous vehicles, and from natural language processing to predictive analytics, these advancements have made AI more accessible and practical for a wide range of industries and use cases.

Neural Networks and Their Enhancements

The contemporary landscape of AI is fundamentally built upon the concept of neural networks, especially deep learning networks, which are designed to emulate the structure and functionality of the human brain. These networks have evolved remarkably, leading to significant advancements in AI's capability and range of applications. One of the pivotal enhancements in this field has been the development of specific neural network architectures like convolutional neural networks (CNNs) and recurrent neural networks (RNNs). CNNs have become instrumental in image recognition tasks, enabling AI to interpret and process visual data with unprecedented accuracy. RNNs, on the other hand, excel in handling sequential data, making them ideal for tasks that involve time-series analysis or language processing.

Further revolutionizing AI's potential, the advent of attention mechanisms and transformer models has marked a significant milestone, particularly in the field of natural language processing (NLP). These innovations allow AI systems to handle and interpret human language more effectively, enabling a range of applications from automated translation services to advanced chatbots. Transformers, for instance, have been a game-changer in understanding and generating human-like text, contributing significantly to the development of more sophisticated AI-driven language models.

These advancements in neural networks and AI architectures have not only expanded AI's practical applications but also opened new avenues for research and development. AI can now tackle complex tasks that were once thought to be exclusively within the realm of human capability. From healthcare diagnostics to autonomous vehicles, the impact of these neural network enhancements is widespread, reshaping industries and revolutionizing the way we interact with technology. The continuous evolution of these technologies promises even more groundbreaking developments in AI, potentially leading to more intuitive, efficient, and human-like AI systems in the future.

Large Language Models (LLMs) and Artificial General Intelligence (AGI)

A significant milestone in the field of AI has been the development and commercial deployment of Large Language Models (LLMs), such as OpenAI's GPT (Generative Pre-trained Transformer) series. These models represent a leap forward in AI's ability to process and generate human language. Trained on extensive datasets, LLMs can produce text that is not only coherent but also contextually relevant. This capability makes them highly versatile tools, finding applications in a multitude of areas including automated content generation, conversational agents for customer service, and even in creative writing.

The impact of these models extends beyond their immediate applications. They serve as a foundation for exploring more advanced AI concepts, particularly the notion of Artificial General Intelligence (AGI). AGI represents an AI system with the ability to understand, learn, and apply its intelligence across a broad range of tasks, mirroring human cognitive abilities. While AGI is currently more a theoretical ambition than a practical reality, the progress in LLMs and deep learning technologies provides a glimpse into a future where AGI could be actualized much sooner than anyone realizes.

In fact, it should be noted that some experts believe that organizations like OpenAI have already created limited deployments of AGI. It is speculated that the controversy centered around the firing and then rehiring of OpenAI's co-founder and CEO Sam Altman was related to OpenAI's development of AGI and the Board of Directors caution on its general release.

The prospect of developing and deploying an AGI raises both excitement and caution within the scientific community and beyond. As suggested, the advancements suggest that the realization of AGI might be closer than previously anticipated. However, this also brings to light the need for preparedness in addressing the ethical, societal, and regulatory implications of such a powerful technology. The development of AGI could redefine our interaction with machines, leading to profound changes in various aspects of life, including work, education, and daily activities. As such, there is a growing discourse on ensuring responsible development and deployment of these technologies, to harness their benefits while mitigating potential risks.

The Rapid Adoption of OpenAI's ChatGPT

OpenAI's introduction of ChatGPT on November 30, 2022, marked a significant milestone in making AI more accessible to the general public. This event was akin to the launch of the iPhone times 1000X. ChatGPT's launch unleashing an unstoppable transformative force that showcased to the world the potential of AI to affect everyday life. ChatGPT's rapid ascent in popularity was nothing short of meteoric. Within just five days of its launch, it attracted over 1 million users, a number that soared to 100 million within 90 days. Remarkably, before its first anniversary, ChatGPT had already amassed a global user base of 200 million, underscoring its widespread appeal and utility.

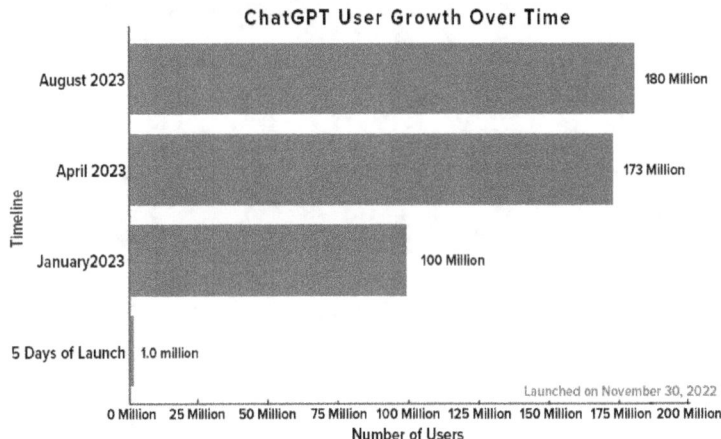

https://nerdynav.com/chatgpt-statistics/

ChatGPT-3, built upon a highly sophisticated Large Language Model (LLM), demonstrated an unprecedented level of natural language interaction, exhibiting a deep understanding and contextual awareness that was previously unseen in AI applications. Its success catalyzed a flurry of activity in the AI sphere, prompting numerous other tech giants and startups to launch their own LLMs. Competitors such as Google with Gemini, X with Grok, Anthropic with Claude, Meta with LLaMA, and Alibaba with Tongyi Qianwen, have since introduced their versions of advanced LLMs. Furthermore, announcements from other major players like Apple, Baidu, and Nvidia indicate a growing and competitive field. AI driven Image generation tools from Midjourney, OpenAI, Adobe and others launched simultaneously, providing increased momentum to the AI transformative wave that hit in 2023.

This wave of LLM development signifies a broader trend in AI technology, reflecting an increased focus on natural language processing capabilities. As these models become more sophisticated and widespread, they promise to further integrate AI into various aspects of daily life and work, potentially revolutionizing how we interact with technology and access information. The rapid expansion of LLMs also highlights the need to act quickly to expand discussions about the ethical, societal, and practical implications of these powerful AI tools.

Chapter 2: Transforming Work and the Workforce

As Artificial Intelligence, epitomized by advanced platforms like ChatGPT, continues to evolve, it presents a multifaceted impact on various sectors, symbolizing both a boon and a challenge for the workforce. AI's ability to automate tasks, previously considered within the realm of human intellect, showcases its potential to significantly enhance efficiency and drive innovation. However, this technological advancement also brings forth considerable challenges to traditional job roles and the overall structure of the workforce.

Beyond mere task automation, AI's capabilities extend to groundbreaking developments in critical sectors. One of the most significant benefits of AI is its role in accelerating the development of new drugs and life-saving medical treatments. By analyzing vast datasets and identifying patterns beyond human capability, AI aids in faster and more efficient drug discovery processes, potentially reducing time and costs associated with bringing new medications to market.

In the realm of environmental sustainability, AI is playing a pivotal role in the development of new clean energy technologies. By optimizing energy consumption and enhancing the efficiency of renewable energy systems, AI contributes to the fight against climate change. Moreover, AI-driven solutions are revolutionizing manufacturing and delivery processes, enabling more efficient production methods and reducing waste, thereby contributing to a more sustainable global economy.

While AI brings these substantial benefits, it is essential to acknowledge and address the challenges it poses to the workforce. The displacement of jobs due to AI-driven automation necessitates a rethinking of job roles and a focus on reskilling and upskilling initiatives. The future of work in an AI-dominated landscape will likely hinge on finding a balance between leveraging AI's transformative potential and mitigating its disruptive effects on employment. This delicate equilibrium calls for strategic planning, policy intervention, and a collaborative effort between various stakeholders to harness AI's benefits while ensuring a sustainable and inclusive future for the workforce.

AI's Dichotomy: Augmentation vs. Displacement

On one hand, AI stands as a formidable tool for enhancing human capabilities, opening up avenues for unprecedented creativity and efficiency. It functions as a dynamic force for innovation, transforming various industries by integrating human skills with the precision and speed of machines. This synergistic combination paves the way for breakthroughs in numerous fields, from healthcare diagnostics to sophisticated data analysis, fostering advancements that were once beyond reach.

On the other hand, AI's rapid progression also brings with it the shadow of job displacement. As AI systems become increasingly capable of performing tasks traditionally executed by humans, from routine administrative duties to more complex decision-making roles, there is a growing concern over job obsolescence. This shift necessitates a fundamental reassessment of workforce structures and employment paradigms. It calls for a proactive approach in reimagining the future of work, where reskilling and upskilling become central to workforce development strategies.

The challenge lies in striking a balance between leveraging AI's transformative potential and mitigating its impact on employment. This involves not only adapting existing roles to coexist with AI but also creating new job categories that emerge from AI-driven changes. The path forward requires a concerted effort from policymakers, educators, and industry

14

leaders to ensure that the workforce is prepared for this new era, characterized by the coexistence of human intelligence and artificial intelligence.

The Multifaceted Impact of AI on the Job Market

The impact of AI on the job market is multifaceted and significant, particularly as AI technologies become more advanced and integrated into various sectors. In customer service, for example, AI's presence is already making a notable difference. Chatbots and virtual assistants are managing high volumes of customer inquiries with increasing efficiency. This trend not only reduces the need for human customer service representatives but also indicates a future where sophisticated AI, especially with the development of advanced large language models, could further minimize human involvement in these roles.

The statistics regarding AI-induced job displacement are striking and paint a picture of the substantial changes that the workforce might face in the near future. According to a report by McKinsey & Company[1,2]:

- Globally, approximately 85 million jobs could be replaced by automation by 2025 and 300 million over the next decade.
- In the United States alone, around 39 million jobs are at risk of being automated by AI by 2030.
- Across various professions, an estimated 2,000 work activities are susceptible to automation, spanning over 800 different job roles.
- AI has the capacity to automate as much as 81% of the tasks currently performed in various workplaces.
- By 2030, it is projected that AI could automate up to 50% of the time currently spent on work-related tasks.

Let these statistics sink in.

These statistics underscore the transformative potential of AI in reshaping the job market. The increasing ability of AI to perform tasks traditionally done by humans signifies a shift towards a more automated future. This transformation is not limited to low-skill, repetitive jobs but encompasses a range of professions, including those that require complex decision-making skills. The ripple effect of this shift in the labor market is vast, affecting everything from economic structures to individual livelihoods. As AI continues to advance, it's becoming increasingly crucial for industries, policymakers, and educational institutions to prepare for these changes. Strategies need to be developed for workforce adaptation, including reskilling programs and educational reforms, to ensure that the workforce can thrive in an AI-dominated future.

The magnitude of these statistics from McKinsey & Company highlights a pressing need for a proactive approach to managing AI's integration into the workforce. It is not just about adapting to the changes but also about harnessing the potential of AI to create new job opportunities and improve productivity and efficiency in the workplace. The challenge lies in balancing the benefits of automation with the socio-economic impact of job displacement, ensuring a smooth transition into the evolving job market landscape. This transition will require collaboration across sectors, innovative policy solutions, and a shared vision for a future where AI complements and enhances human capabilities in the workforce.

The Economic Incentives that Drive AI Adoption

The adoption of AI across various industries is not just a technological trend but also an economic strategy driven by substantial financial incentives. A pivotal study conducted in 2023 by Harvard[3], in collaboration with Boston Consulting Group (BCG), revealed some compelling data regarding the benefits of AI's implementation. The study found that BCG consultants using AI completed 12.2% more tasks while doing it 25.1% faster. They also produced over 40% higher quality results compared to those not using AI. These remarkable figures indicate that for every dollar spent on AI automation, firms could expect to achieve a return of three to four dollars in savings or tangible benefits. These savings are attributed to increased efficiency, reduced operational costs, and enhanced productivity resulting from AI adoption.

This significant ROI has motivated many CEOs, as highlighted in PwC's Annual Global CEO Survey, to plan considerable job reductions in their organizations by the end of 2024, attributing these cuts to AI automation. The survey underscores a growing trend among business leaders to leverage AI for economic gains, aligning their operational strategies with AI-driven solutions.

Further studies and reports have corroborated these findings, underscoring the economic rationale behind AI deployment. For instance, research by McKinsey & Company has shown that AI can potentially deliver up to $2 trillion in additional value in manufacturing and supply chain planning[4].

Similarly, a report by Accenture revealed that AI could boost profitability by an average of 38% across 16 industries by 2035[5]. These projections are based on AI's ability to streamline operations, enhance customer experiences, and innovate product and service offerings.

The economic incentive for AI adoption extends beyond mere cost savings. AI is reshaping business models, enabling companies to tap into new markets, create innovative products and services, and stay competitive in a rapidly evolving digital landscape. As such, the decision to integrate AI is increasingly seen not just as a technological upgrade but as a strategic investment essential for long-term business sustainability and growth.

In summary, the economic incentives for AI adoption are clear and compelling. With substantial ROI, increased profitability, and enhanced competitive advantage, AI is set to remain a key driver of business strategy and economic growth in various industries. However, as organizations navigate this transition, it is crucial to balance these economic benefits with considerations of workforce impact and ethical implications, ensuring a holistic and sustainable approach to AI integration.

"AI is already changing our world, and experts have repeatedly told us that it will have a profound impact on everything from our national security to our classrooms to our workforce, including potentially significant job displacement," - Senator Chuck Schumer

https://www.reuters.com/technology/us-senate-leader-schedules-classified-ai-briefings-2023-06-06/

Chapter 3: Case Study - Deciding to Augment or Displace Your Workforce

The following is a Real-World AI Case Study of one firms decision on whether to Augment or Displace its workforce with AI.

In the bustling heart of New York City, a boutique creative marketing firm stood at a critical crossroads in mid-2023. Known for its exceptional talent in graphic design and creative marketing, the firm, led by a visionary CEO, recognized the inexorable rise of Artificial Intelligence (AI) in the dynamic marketing landscape. Faced with the choice of augmenting or displacing its workforce with AI, the CEO contemplated a decision that would redefine the firm's future.

The AI Workforce Augmentation Assessment

Understanding the need for a strategic approach to AI, the CEO engaged AIworkforce.org, a specialized consulting firm, to conduct an AI Workforce Assessment. The aim was to integrate AI tools like Midjourney, DALLE-3, Adobe Firefly, and ChatGPT into their creative processes and understand new AI tools and their impact on productivity and quality.

Unveiling AI's Dual Nature

The assessment brought to light the transformative power of AI, showcasing its ability to significantly boost productivity and enhance quality. However, it also revealed a challenging truth: the potential reduction in the need for human creatives. The firm's CEO faced the profound question of balancing innovation with the ethical considerations of workforce displacement.

The Pivotal Decision

After much deliberation, in mid-2023, the CEO made the difficult decision to reduce the firm's staff by 30%. This decision, while painful, was seen as essential for keeping pace with competitors and embracing innovation. The remaining team members were provided extensive AI training, equipping them to effectively use AI tools in augmenting their creative skills.

The Ethical Dilemma of Innovation

The choice to reduce staff was not taken lightly, as it involved letting go of talented individuals who were more than employees—they were part of a close-knit community. Yet, the CEO recognized that failing to adapt could lead to stagnation and regression in a rapidly evolving market.

Thriving in an AI-Driven Era

The decision to embrace AI has transformed the marketing firm. Although reduced in size, the firm has become more competitive in terms of cost and creativity. AI has not only become a tool for innovation but a catalyst for a new era of enhanced creativity and efficiency.

Reflection for the Readers

This case study invites readers to ponder a critical question: If faced with a similar situation, what decision would you make? As AI continues to reshape industries, business leaders must navigate the delicate balance between AI augmentation and workforce displacement, making choices that will shape the future of their organizations, their industries, and our society.

Chapter 4: AI and the Transformation of the Job Market

As AI continues its unprecedented trajectory of growth, the imperative to ethically navigate its landscape becomes increasingly pronounced. The rapid enhancement of AI capabilities, spurred by technological advancements and the widespread adoption of tools like ChatGPT, raises critical ethical concerns. These concerns revolve around ensuring fair and responsible use, maintaining accountability, and upholding transparency in AI-driven processes and decisions.

While AI is estimated to generate as many as 97 million jobs over the next decade[6], it also stands to replace three to four jobs for every new one it creates. This disparity highlights the urgent need for strategic workforce planning and the development of new skill sets to keep pace with AI's evolution.

In this evolving landscape, it is imperative to strike a balance between harnessing AI's potential for economic growth and innovation and mitigating its impact on job displacement. Navigating this terrain calls for a concerted effort from policymakers, industry leaders, and the global community to craft strategies that support workforce transitions, foster skill development, and ensure ethical AI deployment for a sustainable and equitable future.

The Emerging Challenge in the Labor Market

The rapid advancement of technologies like self-driving and autonomous systems is precipitating a significant ethical dilemma: the displacement of jobs by AI. This issue is particularly acute in sectors such as the trucking industry, which is a vital component of the U.S. economy, employing approximately 1.8 million truck drivers[7]. The potential for widespread adoption of self-driving technology on U.S. highways signals a profound shift, affecting not just the technological landscape but supply chains, the cost of goods, inflation and even the overall economy. In the following section of the book, we dive into the Trucking Industry in order to provide a better understanding of the potential impact of AI on a specific industry and group of workers. Later in this chapter we will explore AI's impact on a dozen other industries and professions each of which is impacted differently, all of which will experience large scale reductions of overall workforces as a result of AI.

A Spotlight on The Trucking Industry and Truck Drivers

The trucking industry is a prime example of where AI technology could entirely supplant a human skill set over time. The shift to autonomous driving is set to fundamentally transform employment dynamics within this sector. Consider the typical profile of union long-haul truck drivers in America: predominantly middle-aged men, with an average age of around 52 years, earning approximately $100,000 annually, including benefits[8]. Transitioning to self-driving technology, which is estimated to cost less than $12,000 per year, presents trucking companies with a staggering 88% annual saving in labor costs. For CEOs of large trucking firms, the day self-driving technology is approved for use on U.S highways by federal regulators, embracing automation becomes a survival strategy rather than just an option. Hesitation or failure to adopt this technology could mean falling behind competitors and risking the company's viability.

This shift to autonomous trucks is expected to be both rapid and widespread. If automated technology replaces even 20% of the driving jobs in its initial years of deployment, this could affect 360,000 drivers and their families. Families that are dependent on incomes from the trucking industry to pay their mortgages, car loans, and other financial commitments. The critical question is: What preparations are being made for this foreseeable shift in the transportation sector of the U.S workforce? The potential mass displacement of truck drivers raises profound societal questions. How will this large group of individuals collectively respond to losing their jobs to AI? Will there be sufficient opportunities for retraining, allowing them to transition to roles with comparable income? Or might there be a negative, even disruptive, reaction to such a sudden change? Scenarios such as thousands or even tens of thousands of truck drivers peacefully protesting or maybe not so peacefully protesting by blockading major bridges and highways, thereby disrupting the flow of goods, and the U.S economy. We should remember the Canadian Truck Drivers response to mandated COVID vaccines. These possibilities point to the need for proactive measures and policies to manage the transition.

Chapter 5: The Imminent Reality of AI's Impact on Specific Careers

The trucking industry is just one example of how AI-induced automation could reshape the job market. Across various sectors, from manufacturing to retail, similar patterns of displacement are emerging. The adoption of AI is leading to significant cost savings for businesses but at the potential cost of widespread job losses. It should be noted that AI will create millions of new jobs, and will result in an increase in income to certain jobs; however, the following is an analysis of how AI will impact certain jobs over the next decade.

Accounting and Audit Services

Accounting, a profession traditionally reliant on meticulousness and precision, is on the brink of a significant transformation due to AI. Nearly 90% of accounting tasks, from data entry and reconciliation to complex financial reporting and auditing, can be automated by AI. Advanced AI systems are capable of processing vast amounts of financial data with greater accuracy and at a fraction of the time it takes humans. This automation promises increased efficiency and reduced error rates, but it also implies a substantial reduction in the need for human accountants for routine tasks. AI's integration in accounting could lead to a restructuring of the profession, where the role of accountants evolves into analysts or strategists, focusing more on managing clients and interpreting AI-processed data and less on data entry and report generation. According to the U.S. Department of Labor, as of 2022 there were 1.4 million[9] accountants and auditors employed in the United States. It is estimated that 50% of accountants and auditors will be displaced by AI automation over the next decade.

Legal Services: Redefining Law Practice

In the legal sector, AI stands to revolutionize the way legal work is conducted. Approximately 60% of legal work is spent on research and contract review, tasks that AI can perform with higher speed and efficiency. AI technology will soon be more proficient than humans when it comes to analyzing legal documents, writing contracts, and even offering preliminary legal advice. While AI might not replace the nuanced judgment and advocacy of experienced attorneys, it will automate many functions within a law firm. This shift will lead to fewer opportunities for paralegals and junior lawyers, whose tasks are more susceptible to automation. The legal profession will likely see a shift in focus, with lawyers spending less time on research and routine documentation and more on strategy, negotiations, and courtroom advocacy, areas where human skills are irreplaceable by AI.

According to the U.S. Department of Labor, as of 2022 there were 1.33 million[10] lawyers employed in the United States. Ultimately it is estimated that 50% of lawyers and staff currently employed in U.S law firms will be replaced by AI automation by the end of the decade.

Architecture: AI in Design and Drafting

In architecture, AI's impact is set to be profound. AI can draft, draw, design, and create architectural drawings and schematics faster and more accurately than humans. This capability means that up to 80% of tasks completed by architectural firms can potentially be automated by 2025. AI tools can quickly generate design alternatives based on specific criteria, perform structural analysis, and even predict materials costs, streamlining the design process. Custom AI that are currently in development can ensure that designs are drawn to local building code specifications and will even create documentation needed for local building permits. It is however unlikely that the role of architects disappears. It is very likely that the role evolves significantly. Architects may in the future focus more on the creative and conceptual aspects of design, client interaction, and project oversight, while AI handles the technical and repetitive aspects. One thing for certain is that the number of architects and architectural firms will dramatically diminish over the next decade as AI capabilities in the field are enhanced by custom built AI.

According to the National Council of Architectural Registration Boards (NCARB), as of 2020 there were 117,000 Architects employed in the United States[11]. It is estimated that AI's impact will affect 40% of employees in Architecture firms in the U.S by 2030.

Writers, Journalists and Authors

For writers, the advent of sophisticated generative AI poses a significant shift. According to Reuters, much of the role of a Journalist, from research, content creation to editing, can be automated by AI. Generative AI models can produce articles, reports, and even creative literature, challenging the traditional role of journalist, authors and writers. However, the unique voice, creativity, and emotional depth that human writers bring to their work remain difficult for AI to replicate fully for now. The profession might see a greater emphasis on editing, curating, and enhancing AI-generated content, as well as focusing on pieces that require deep insights, emotional intelligence, and original thought.

According to DataUSA.io, there were 173,000 writers and authors employed in the United States in 2022[12]. It is estimated that only 10% of these individuals will be replaced by AI, however it is estimated that AI will have a profound impact on their earning ability. It is estimated that the average annual income of writers and authors in the U.S will decline by as much as 30% over the next decade as a result of AI.

Software Development: AI's Role in Coding

In software development, tools like GitHub Copilot demonstrate AI's capability to write code faster and more efficiently than humans. In a recent episode of the All-In podcast with Billionaires Chamath Palihapitiya, Jason Calacanis, David Sacks and David Friedberg it was estimated that 80% of software development tasks can be replaced by AI today[13]. AI can automate coding, bug fixing, and even some testing processes, potentially reducing the demand for human developers in certain areas. However, software development is not just about writing code; it involves understanding user needs, creativity in design, and strategic planning, aspects where human developers will continue to play a crucial role. The profession will inevitably see a shift towards Human and AI collaboration where more complex and creative aspects of software development are led by talented human developers, and where routine coding tasks are handled by AI.

In 2022, the U.S. Department of Labor reported 1.53 million software developers in the workforce[14]. However, a seismic shift is on the horizon due to AI's burgeoning role in software development. By 2025, it's projected that AI will replace over 50% of human-led software development tasks. This significant transition is anticipated to drastically reduce software development costs by 50% to 80%, marking AI as a profoundly deflationary force within the industry.

This shift carries substantial implications for employment in the sector. Estimates suggest that more than 500,000 software developers in the U.S. might lose their jobs due to AI integration. Moreover, the remaining developers might face a reduction in income, potentially up to 50%, by the end of the decade. The increasing capability of AI to autonomously write software stands to not only reshape the industry's cost structure but also redefine the job market and earning potential within this field.

Customer Service Representatives: AI in Customer Interaction

AI is significantly impacting the field of customer service. Chatbots and virtual assistants can handle a vast array of customer inquiries, reducing the need for human customer service representatives.

By automating mundane tasks, AI could provide a better experience for customers with more self-service options and help fix some of the industry's biggest problems, especially employee burnout and inefficiency. Working in customer service is notoriously stressful—it was named one of the world's top 10 most stressful jobs—and companies see turnover rates of up to 45% of agents every year. That has led to a massive talent shortage and is costly for companies to continually recruit and train new employees—all of which affects the customer and employee experience.

Conversely, AI systems can provide quick responses, handle multiple queries simultaneously, and are available 24/7, enhancing customer experience while reducing operational costs. However, complex customer issues requiring empathy, negotiation, and deep problem-solving will still need human intervention. The role of customer service representatives may evolve to focus on these more complex interactions and on overseeing and training AI systems. This represents only 20% of current workloads. According to the U.S Department of Labor, there were 2.98 million Customer Service Representatives working in the U.S in 2022[15]. It is estimated that at least 70% of the tasks currently performed by CSRs could be replaced by AI by the end of the decade. The impact to the U.S labor force would be a loss of over 2 million jobs.

AI's Encroachment

Across just these specific professions, according to U.S. government statistics, there were approximately 9.7 million workers employed in these careers in 2022. AI's encroachment into these professions and various others signifies a paradigm shift in the job market. While AI brings efficiencies and innovations, it also necessitates a rethinking of job roles and employment structures. Across these professions, the common theme is the transition from routine, repetitive tasks to roles that require more creative, strategic, and interpersonal skills. As AI takes over more functions, the value in human-centric skills such as emotional intelligence, creativity, and complex problem-solving becomes more pronounced.

The challenge for industries and educators alike is to anticipate these changes and prepare the workforce accordingly. This involves not only equipping people with the skills to work alongside AI but also fostering adaptability and lifelong learning as core competencies. For policymakers, the focus should be on creating frameworks that support this transition, mitigate the negative impacts of job displacement, and ensure that the benefits of AI are broadly shared across society.

As AI continues to evolve and become more ingrained in various fields, the narrative is not just about job loss but also about transformation and adaptation. The future will likely see a blend of human and machine capabilities, with AI augmenting human work rather than completely replacing it. This future requires a proactive approach, embracing the opportunities AI presents while addressing its challenges head-on. The ultimate goal is to create a future where AI enhances human capabilities and contributes to a more efficient, creative, and equitable world.

One such example of how AI is now enhancing human capabilities, creating new opportunities, and truly changing the world is a recent discovery by Google's DeepMind. In November 2023, Google DeepMind announced that it had trained a deep learning AI model to predict the structure of over 2.2 million crystalline materials - 45 times more than the number discovered in the history of science. To put this in perspective, the AI developed by Google DeepMind achieved an order of magnitude expansion in stable materials known to humanity, finding 800 years' worth of new materials, many with revolutionary potential, in just a few weeks. From these 2.2 million materials more than 380,000 could be useful for everything from creating new battery technology to developing new superconductors.

Chapter 6: The Ethical Balancing Act of AI Created Opportunities and Challenges

The dawn of the AI era has ushered in a new paradigm in the global workforce. Artificial Intelligence, with its unprecedented computational power and learning capabilities, is redefining the nature of jobs across various sectors. This transition, marked by both innovative prospects and significant challenges, is reshaping the employment landscape in profound ways. The proliferation of AI technologies offers the potential for creating new job categories, enhancing productivity, and propelling industries into new frontiers of efficiency and innovation. However, this technological revolution also raises critical ethical questions, particularly concerning job displacement and the equitable distribution of AI's benefits.

PwC estimates that 30% of jobs in the United States could be automated by the Mid-2030s.[17]

Goldman Sachs reports that 2 out of 3 jobs in the U.S. and Europe is exposed to some degree of AI Automation.[18]

AI's integration into the workforce is a multifaceted phenomenon, significantly impacting diverse demographic groups. It presents a unique set of opportunities and challenges that require careful consideration and strategic adaptation. This chapter delves into the nuanced implications of AI on different segments of the workforce, exploring the ethical responsibilities of integrating AI in a manner that balances technological advancement with societal welfare.

Delving into Demographic Impacts of AI:

Impact on Women and Minorities

The advancement of AI holds different ramifications for various demographic groups, with women and minorities often facing distinct challenges. Women, for instance, historically underrepresented in technology sectors, may find themselves disproportionately impacted by the automation of jobs. The integration of AI in the workplace also brings to the fore concerns about inherent biases in AI algorithms, potentially perpetuating existing gender and racial disparities. Addressing these issues necessitates not only the careful design of AI systems but also proactive measures to ensure equitable access to AI training and career opportunities for these groups.

Older Workers' Adaptation

Another demographic significantly affected by the AI revolution is older workers. As AI technologies rapidly evolve, older employees may struggle to adapt to new digital tools and AI-driven processes, leading to a potential skills gap. This scenario underscores the need for targeted training programs and lifelong learning initiatives, aimed at enabling older American workers to remain competitive and productive in an increasingly AI-driven job market.

> *Researchers from the University of Pennsylvania and OpenAI found that white-collar workers earning up to $80,000 per year are the most likely to be affected by AI driven workforce automation.*[19]

Lower-Income Individuals and Digital Access

Lower-income individuals, particularly those with limited access to internet and computing technologies, are at risk of being left behind in the AI-driven economic landscape. The digital divide could widen, exacerbating economic inequalities, as those without adequate digital access struggle to benefit from AI-related job growth. Bridging this gap requires concerted efforts to ensure inclusivity in digital infrastructure and education, making AI and its associated educational resources accessible to all demographics.

Forbes says that the future of AI brings endless possibilities and applications that will help largely simplify our lives. It will help shape the future and destiny of humanity positively, whilst Bernard Marr & Co says that the transformation impact of artificial intelligence on our society will have far-reaching economic, legal, political, and regulatory implications on all jobs and industries that we need to be discussing and preparing for. One thing is for certain, the impact of AI will not be felt equally by all demographic groups. This highlights the need for inclusive strategies and policies that ensure the equitable distribution of AI's benefits and mitigate its potential to exacerbate existing societal disparities.

Chapter 7: AI's Deflationary Impact

According to the Federal Reserve Bank, the Total Wages and Salaries paid in the United States in 2022 were $10.5 Trillion[20]. The total U.S workforce in 2022 was 164.3 million workers[21].

The potential economic impact of AI automation, particularly in the context of its effects on inflation and deflation, is a subject of considerable debate. To analyze these claims and draw a conclusion, it's essential to consider various factors:

Job Displacement and Wage Pressure Impact on Inflations

AI-driven automation is expected to displace a significant number of jobs. This displacement, particularly in sectors like transportation (due to autonomous driving), customer services, and retail, could lead to an increase in unemployment. Higher unemployment generally exerts downward pressure on wages as the labor supply exceeds demand. Lower wages could lead to reduced consumer spending, which in turn might cause deflationary pressure in the economy.

Cost Reduction in Goods and Services

AI and automation lead to efficiency gains and cost reductions in producing goods and services. For instance, autonomous driving reduces transportation and shipping costs, and AI in retail leading to more efficient operations with self-checkouts and computer vision, potentially lowering the prices of goods. Lower production costs can translate to lower prices for consumers, contributing to deflationary trends.

Increased Competition and Competitive Pricing

With AI-enhanced efficiency, businesses might engage in more competitive pricing to attract customers, further contributing to deflationary pressures. For example, law firms employing AI tools may lower their fees due to increased efficiency and competition, affecting the overall pricing in the sector.

Consumption Patterns and Demand

The role of AI in changing consumption patterns is also crucial. If job losses lead to decreased disposable income among large segments of the population, there could be a decline in consumer demand. A decrease in demand can contribute to deflation. However, if AI leads to new job creation in other sectors, especially high-tech, pharmaceutical, and clean energy sectors, this could offset some of the deflationary pressures by creating new economic opportunities and driving demand.

Government Policies and Fiscal Responses

How governments respond to AI-induced economic shifts is critical. Policies aimed at mitigating job losses, such as retraining programs, unemployment benefits, or stimulus measures, can influence whether the economy experiences inflation or deflation. Effective policy responses could stimulate demand and counter deflationary trends.

Long-Term Economic Growth Amidst AI-Induced Job Displacement

As we grapple with estimates suggesting the loss of 300 to 375 million jobs due to AI in the next decade, it's imperative to consider the role of AI in long-term economic growth. While there is valid concern about job displacement, AI-driven industries like research, robotics, and AI integration services are poised for growth. However, realizing the potential for long-term economic expansion requires proactive and inclusive planning by governments, corporate leaders, and policymakers. Developing global and inclusive strategies today is crucial for harnessing AI's transformative power. These strategies should encompass creating new job sectors, retraining the workforce for AI-enhanced roles, and fostering a culture of continuous learning and innovation.

Conclusion: Navigating AI's Economic Impact

The prospect of AI-induced job displacement presents a significant challenge, yet it also opens doors to new opportunities. While the short-term effects might lean towards deflationary trends due to job losses and cost reductions, the long-term economic landscape can be shaped positively by AI. This requires a strategic approach, focusing on developing new industries, re-skilling workers, and implementing inclusive policies that consider the broader societal impact. The key lies in global collaboration and proactive planning. By embracing these challenges and opportunities, we can steer the course of AI's impact towards sustainable economic growth and a future where technology and human ingenuity coalesce for the betterment of all.

Chapter 8: Policy and Ethical Considerations in AI Integration

The integration of AI across various sectors raises important policy and ethical considerations. Governments and regulatory bodies face the challenge of developing policies that not only foster innovation but also ensure the ethical use of AI. This includes establishing standards for data privacy, addressing potential biases in AI algorithms, and ensuring transparency in AI-driven decisions.

Policies should aim to bridge the digital divide, ensuring equitable access to AI technologies and training. This is particularly crucial in ensuring that advancements in AI do not exacerbate existing social and economic inequalities. Furthermore, policies need to support the workforce transitioning from traditional roles to new AI-driven opportunities. A key aspect of such policies is to facilitate effective retraining programs, especially for sectors heavily affected by AI. This retraining should focus on equipping the workforce with the necessary skills to thrive in an AI-augmented job market.

Ethical AI Deployment

Ethical considerations in AI deployment are paramount. AI systems must be developed and utilized in ways that consider societal implications, especially regarding employment and workforce dynamics. This necessitates a human-centric approach in AI development, emphasizing AI's role in augmenting human work rather than replacing it. Ethical AI deployment involves ensuring that AI systems do not perpetuate biases and that their decisions are transparent and accountable.

This ethical approach requires collaborative efforts among policymakers, industry leaders, and technologists to develop AI technologies that are not only innovative but also socially responsible. Such an approach ensures that the benefits of AI are distributed equitably across society, mitigating the risks of widening social and economic disparities.

Case Studies and Futuristic Outlook of AI's Role in Accelerating Research & Development

AI is a driving force in reshaping sectors like pharmaceuticals, medical research, and clean energy, heralding a new era of innovation and employment. In the pharmaceutical industry, AI accelerates drug discovery and development, rapidly bringing critical health solutions to fruition. Its role in personalized medicine is transforming treatment approaches, leading to burgeoning careers in bioinformatics and genetic research.

Similarly, medical research is undergoing a paradigm shift with AI's intervention. AI's prowess in data analysis aids in refining diagnostic accuracy and fostering innovative treatment methodologies, giving rise to new hybrid roles combining healthcare and technology expertise.

In the realm of clean energy, AI is a crucial player in optimizing energy usage and fostering sustainable solutions. This is increasingly important in global efforts against climate change. AI's contributions to enhancing energy efficiency, advancing renewable energy, and reducing emissions are paving the way for new job opportunities in green technology and environmental sustainability.

Ultimately, as we look towards the future, AI's role in accelerating research and development is poised to be a cornerstone of technological progress and societal advancement. AI's potential in transforming industries, creating new job roles, and addressing pressing global challenges underscores its significance in our evolving world. However, as we embrace these advancements, it is imperative to navigate this journey ethically, ensuring equitable access to the benefits AI brings and mitigating any potential disparities it may create. The future with AI promises not just technological transformation but also a redefinition of work and innovation, demanding a holistic approach that balances advancement with ethical responsibility. As we step into this AI-augmented era, our focus should remain on harnessing AI's power for the greater good, while continually adapting to its ever-evolving landscape.

Chapter 9: From Cloning to AI: Drawing Ethical Lines in Technological Sands

The ethical debate surrounding AI mirrors historical discussions on cloning. Just as the scientific community has developed the ability to clone animals and potentially humans, yet globally decided to impose ethical constraints on this practice, similar considerations are now required for AI. The dilemma lies in whether certain AI capabilities, particularly those that could lead to massive job displacements, should be restricted on ethical grounds. This comparison calls for a conscientious evaluation of AI's potential societal impact, weighing technological advancement against ethical implications. The question becomes: Should we limit AI technologies that, although technically feasible, pose significant ethical and societal concerns, akin to the restrictions placed on cloning for ethical reasons? These parallel highlights the need for a global consensus on responsible AI development, ensuring that technology serves humanity's best interests without causing detrimental societal disruptions.

As we embark on a critical examination of the multifaceted risks associated with AI in our modern world, we delve into twenty potential dangers that AI poses, offering a comprehensive analysis of each threat and its broader implications for individuals, societies, and global stability. These twenty potential dangers are just a subset of all the possible risks that can come from the widespread deployment of AI.

As AI continues to weave itself into the fabric of our daily existence, enhancing efficiency and pioneering innovations, it also opens the door to various ethical challenges. Leaders and Policymakers must explore the manipulation of public discourse through DeepFakes and AI-generated misinformation, highlighting the threats to privacy, democratic values, and ethical norms. There must be widespread scrutiny of the potential of AI in driving biased decision-making across crucial sectors like employment and law enforcement, raising critical questions about fairness and justice.

As we investigate the unprecedented ability of AI in processing personal data, addressing concerns of privacy erosion, data theft, and invasive surveillance, there arises widespread concerns of AI's capabilities in reshaping the landscape of personal security and privacy.

Moving to the financial domain, regulators must examine AI's potential misuse in market manipulation and insider trading, underlining the risks to economic stability and fairness. The weaponization of AI in autonomous weaponry and cybersecurity is also critically assessed, presenting alarming scenarios of unaccountable warfare and sophisticated cyber threats.

Beyond these, AI's impact on labor markets, the propagation of fake news, and manipulation of social media narratives, pose profound risks to employment, public trust, and social cohesion.

Chapter 10: Potential Risks Exacerbated by AI

Here are just a few of the many potential risks that could be exacerbated by AI.

Deepfake Propagated Misinformation

Deepfakes, sophisticated AI-generated videos or audio recordings that convincingly depict real people saying or doing things they never did, pose a serious risk in spreading misinformation. They can be used to create false narratives or manipulate public opinion, impacting politics, social discourse, and individual reputations. The realistic nature of Deepfakes makes it challenging for viewers to distinguish between genuine and fabricated content, thus exacerbating the spread of false information and potentially leading to widespread misinformation and trust issues in media and public figures.

AI Enhanced Mass Surveillance

The utilization of Artificial Intelligence in mass surveillance represents a significant privacy risk. AI's capability to process and analyze vast amounts of data enables the tracking and monitoring of individuals on an unprecedented scale. This raises serious concerns about the potential for abuse, particularly in terms of conducting surveillance without consent. The indiscriminate gathering and analysis of personal data by AI systems threaten individual privacy rights and can lead to unauthorized and invasive scrutiny of personal lives. This aspect of AI underscores the urgent need for stringent privacy protections and ethical guidelines in its deployment.

Personal Data Theft

Artificial Intelligence's advanced data processing capabilities pose a significant risk to personal data security. The technology's ability to analyze and access large datasets can lead to substantial theft of sensitive personal information. This includes crucial financial details and identity data, making individuals vulnerable to identity theft, financial fraud, and privacy breaches. The ease and scale at which AI can potentially harvest and misuse personal data underscores the urgent need for stringent data protection measures and ethical AI practices to safeguard individual privacy.

Manipulating Financial Markets

The use of AI in manipulating financial markets presents a substantial risk. AI's capacity for analyzing vast amounts of data can be exploited for insider trading, offering unfair financial advantages to certain individuals or entities. Furthermore, AI can be used to manipulate market trends, potentially leading to significant economic instability. This misuse not only undermines the fairness and integrity of financial markets but also poses a threat to the overall stability of global economies. Addressing this risk requires stringent regulatory oversight and ethical guidelines to prevent AI from being used unethically in financial activities.

Unemployment Surge

The surge in AI-driven automation presents a formidable challenge, with the potential to replace a vast number of human jobs. Without comprehensive social and economic transition plans, this shift could precipitate widespread unemployment and social upheaval. The risk lies in AI's rapid advancement outpacing the development of new job roles and the reskilling of the workforce, creating a void where employment opportunities used to exist. This scenario necessitates urgent strategic planning and policy intervention to mitigate the negative impacts of AI on employment and ensure a smooth transition for affected workers.

AI-Generated Fake News

AI-Generated Fake News represents a significant risk in the digital age. Leveraging advanced AI technologies, it becomes possible to fabricate and disseminate false information rapidly, exacerbating misinformation and societal divisions. This erosion of trust in media sources can undermine public discourse, manipulate opinions, and skew democratic processes. The ease and efficiency with which AI can generate plausible yet false narratives pose a formidable challenge to discerning fact from fiction, necessitating greater vigilance and sophisticated countermeasures to maintain informational integrity in society.

AI Manipulation of Social Media

The risk of AI manipulation of social media lies in AI-powered bots that can distort online discourse. These bots amplify selected viewpoints, creating an imbalanced representation of public opinion. This manipulation not only skews social media narratives but also has the potential to influence political and social issues by creating false trends or suppressing genuine public discourse. The pervasive nature of this AI application raises serious concerns about the integrity of information and democratic processes, highlighting the need for vigilance and stronger regulatory measures in the digital space.

Although this list of Potential Risk Exacerbated by AI is by no means extensive, this book serves as a clarion call for responsible AI deployment, urging policymakers, industry leaders, and the global community to establish ethical guidelines and robust regulatory frameworks. It seeks to educate those of a pending title wave of change, opportunities and risks related to it emphasizes the need for a balanced approach to AI development, ensuring that while we harness its potential for future advancements, we also safeguard our core values and societal well-being. The exploration of these risks underscores the importance of informed and cautious AI integration, advocating for a future where AI is a force for good, aligning with human interests and ethical standards.

Chapter 11: Policy & Governance in the AI Age

AI Legislation: National and International Approaches

In recent years, the rapid development of AI has necessitated a reevaluation of existing legislative frameworks, prompting both national and international bodies to propose new regulations.

The European Union's AI Act, a pioneering effort in AI legislation, aims to provide a comprehensive legal framework for AI systems across its member states. This Act classifies AI applications based on their risk levels and imposes stringent requirements on high-risk AI systems, particularly those that could significantly impact fundamental rights, such as facial recognition technologies and critical infrastructure AI.

Similarly, the United States has introduced a regulatory framework with President Biden's Executive Order on AI. This order outlines a policy for AI development and use, focusing on maintaining leadership in AI innovation while aligning AI development with democratic values, human rights, and the nation's economic and national security interests. It emphasizes the importance of AI ethics, calling for collaboration between federal agencies, industry, academia, and international partners.

The global landscape of AI legislation is diverse, with countries like Canada, China, and Japan developing their policies reflecting their unique socio-economic contexts. International organizations like the OECD and the United Nations have also been instrumental in facilitating discussions on global AI norms and standards, recognizing the technology's transnational implications.

These legislative efforts highlight the complexities of regulating AI, balancing the need to foster innovation with the protection of public interests and rights. They represent significant steps toward responsible AI development but also underscore the need for ongoing adaptation and refinement of these regulatory frameworks to keep pace with AI's rapid advancements.

Regulatory Challenges and Solutions

The regulatory landscape for AI is fraught with challenges, given the technology's dynamic nature and its broad range of applications. A primary challenge is developing regulations that are both flexible enough to adapt to AI's evolving nature and robust enough to address the various risks it poses.

One key issue is balancing the need to foster innovation with the necessity of maintaining public trust and safety. Over-regulation may stifle AI development and hinder its potential benefits, while under-regulation could lead to ethical breaches, privacy violations, and other harmful outcomes. Policymakers are tasked with finding a middle ground that encourages responsible AI development while protecting societal interests.

Sector-specific regulatory needs are another challenge, as different sectors require tailored approaches due to the specific applications and implications of AI in each field. For instance, healthcare AI demands stringent accuracy and safety standards, while AI in financial services raises concerns about algorithmic transparency and fairness.

Potential solutions include implementing regulatory sandboxes, allowing real-world testing of AI technologies under regulatory oversight to assess risks and benefits in a controlled environment. Another approach is establishing AI governance frameworks within organizations, ensuring AI development and deployment align with ethical standards and legal requirements.

AI Regulation and Privacy Concerns

AI technologies, particularly those involving data processing and analysis, raise significant privacy concerns. Issues like data misuse, surveillance, and unauthorized data access are at the forefront of privacy debates surrounding AI.

The European Union's General Data Protection Regulation (GDPR) addresses privacy in the AI context. GDPR imposes strict data protection requirements, giving individuals more control over their personal data. AI developers and users in the EU must ensure their technologies comply with GDPR principles, including data minimization, consent, and the right to explanation.

As AI systems become more sophisticated, they pose new challenges for privacy protection. For instance, deep learning algorithms can infer sensitive information from seemingly innocuous data, while facial recognition technologies raise concerns about surveillance and individual autonomy.

To mitigate these privacy concerns, a combination of technological solutions, regulatory measures, and public awareness is essential. Privacy-by-design approaches, where privacy safeguards are integrated into AI systems from the outset, are becoming increasingly important. Additionally, there's a need for continuous public dialogue and education on AI and privacy, empowering individuals to understand and advocate for their data rights.

Chapter 12: Understanding the EU's AI Act - What it Means for the Future

On Friday, December 8, 2023, the EU Parliament and Council negotiators reached a provisional agreement on the Artificial Intelligence Act. This regulation aims to ensure that fundamental rights, democracy, the rule of law and environmental sustainability are protected from high-risk AI, while boosting innovation and making Europe a leader in the field. The rules establish obligations for AI based on its potential risks and level of impact.[22]

The European Union's journey towards regulating Artificial Intelligence (AI) culminated in a historic milestone with the AI Act. After extensive deliberation, this groundbreaking legislation is poised to be the world's first comprehensive AI law, setting a precedent for global AI governance.

Key Elements of the EU's AI Act:

1. Risk-Based Approach to AI Regulation:

The AI Act introduces a nuanced risk classification for AI systems, with stringent regulations for high-risk applications in areas like healthcare and public services. This approach aims to balance innovation with the protection of fundamental rights.

2. Transparency and Ethical Standards:

Legally binding rules are set to elevate AI transparency and ethics. Companies must now disclose when users are interacting with AI systems, including chatbots and biometric categorization, and must label AI-generated content like deepfakes.

3. Regulating General Purpose AI:

The Act addresses foundation models, requiring them to meet documentation standards and EU copyright laws. More powerful AI models face stricter regulations, dependent on their computing power, which companies must self-assess.

4. European AI Office for Enforcement:

A new regulatory body, the European AI Office, is established for AI compliance and enforcement, making the EU a pioneer in AI regulation. This office includes an expert panel to advise on AI risks and classification.

5. Significant Fines and Citizen Empowerment:

Noncompliance with the Act can result in substantial fines, ranging from 1.5% to 7% of a company's global sales turnover. Additionally, the Act empowers citizens to file complaints and seek explanations for AI-based decisions.

7. Specific Prohibitions and Law Enforcement Exemptions:

Certain AI applications, such as indiscriminate facial recognition and social scoring, are banned. However, exemptions exist for law enforcement, allowing biometric systems in public spaces under strict conditions and for specific serious crimes.

8. Implementation Timeline and Global Impact:

The finalization and adoption of the AI Act's text are pending. Once in force, there will be a phased implementation timeline for companies, setting a new global standard in AI regulation, similar to the GDPR's influence.

Conclusion:

The EU's AI Act marks an initial attempt by the European Union to strike a balance in regulating the rapidly evolving field of artificial intelligence. It reflects an understanding that as AI technologies continue to develop and permeate various sectors, the need for a regulatory framework becomes increasingly vital.

For businesses, the Act introduces a new landscape of compliance and ethical considerations. Companies, especially those developing or utilizing AI systems, will need to navigate the complexities of risk assessments, transparency requirements, and ethical standards mandated by the Act. This means adapting to new regulations around high-risk AI applications, ensuring transparency in AI interactions, and possibly facing significant fines for non-compliance.

The implications for the business world are multifaceted. On one hand, it might increase operational and compliance costs, especially for smaller enterprises and startups. On the other, it could also drive innovation in AI ethics and safety, potentially leading to more robust and trustworthy AI systems.

Furthermore, the EU's AI Act could set in motion a global trend where other regions might adopt similar regulations, influencing international business operations. Companies operating in the EU or planning to enter the European market will need to align their AI strategies with these new regulations, a process that might require substantial adjustments in their AI development and deployment approaches.

It's important to recognize that the EU's AI Act is a starting point. As the AI industry and technologies continue to evolve, so too will the regulatory landscape. The Act may undergo revisions and updates to keep pace with technological advancements and emerging challenges in the AI sector. This evolving nature of the AI Act signifies the EU's commitment to adapt and respond to the dynamic world of artificial intelligence, aiming to protect citizens while fostering innovation.

In conclusion, the EU's AI Act, in its current form, is an early step in an ongoing journey. It represents an evolving approach to AI governance, one that will likely see refinements and modifications as the world of AI continues to change and expand. Businesses, policymakers, and technologists alike will need to stay agile and informed to navigate this new regulatory environment effectively.

It should be noted that the EU's AI Act protects European privacy and ensures strong social protection for workers but does very little to protect against job displacement as a result of AI automation.

Chapter 13: Decoding President Biden's AI Executive Order on AI

In the realm of artificial intelligence (AI), the United States stands at a crossroads, balancing on the fine line between fostering innovation and ensuring safety and ethical standards. The recent Executive Order on AI by President Biden is a testament to this delicate dance. The directive aims to set the stage for the responsible development and deployment of AI technologies. However, the broad strokes of the order have sparked a debate on the effectiveness of such high-level guidelines in the fast-paced world of AI.

The Executive Order is ambitious in scope, seeking to establish a framework that promotes AI that is safe, secure, and trustworthy. It outlines principles that prioritize safety, security, innovation, competition, and the protection of American interests. Yet, the devil is in the details—or, in this case, the lack thereof. The order provides a broad definition of AI and sets forth principles and priorities, but it stops short of delving into the granular details necessary for practical implementation. This vagueness leaves much open to interpretation, which could lead to a patchwork of enforcement that may hinder rather than help.

The order's broad definition of AI encompasses any machine-based system that makes predictions, recommendations, or decisions. This sweeping categorization includes everything from simple automated decision systems used in loan applications to complex generative AI models that can create realistic synthetic media. The challenge with such a wide net is that it fails to account for the vast differences in risks and implications across various AI applications. Without specific guidance, businesses and developers are left to interpret how to apply these principles to their unique AI systems, which could lead to inconsistent applications of the order's intent.

The potential for a series of legal battles looms large, reminiscent of the government's recent forays into the cryptocurrency sector. The ongoing lawsuit between the Securities and Exchange Commission (SEC) and Ripple over the classification of XRP as a security is a prime example of how broad regulations can lead to protracted legal challenges. Similarly, the AI Executive Order could open the door for the government to interpret AI regulations in various ways, potentially targeting industries and business sectors in an attempt to enforce the order's broad mandates. This approach to regulation raises concerns about the United States' ability to maintain its lead in AI innovation. Countries like China, which have taken a more permissive stance toward AI development, could outpace the U.S. if American companies are bogged down by trying to navigate a complex and uncertain regulatory landscape. The rapid pace of AI development globally means that any attempt to slow progress through regulation may be futile. AI technologies are advancing at breakneck speed, and the international community is not waiting for the U.S. to figure out its regulatory stance.

The Executive Order rightly emphasizes the importance of safety, security, and ethical considerations in AI development. However, the lack of detailed guidance risks creating a regulatory environment that is reactive rather than proactive. Companies may find themselves in a position where they are unsure whether their AI systems comply with the order until they are faced with enforcement actions. This uncertainty could stifle innovation as companies may become overly cautious, slowing down the development of new AI technologies for fear of inadvertently running afoul of the order. Moreover, the order's reliance on existing agencies and their interpretation of its broad principles could lead to a fragmented approach to AI regulation. Different agencies may develop their own standards and guidelines, which could create a confusing and contradictory regulatory environment. This fragmentation could make it difficult for AI developers to ensure that their systems are compliant across different sectors and applications.

The challenge for the government is to act without stifling innovation. It must find a way to provide clear, actionable guidance that allows for the safe and ethical development of AI while also fostering an environment that encourages innovation. The Executive Order is a step in the right direction, but it is just the beginning. The government will need to work closely with industry experts, ethicists, and the AI community to develop detailed regulations that address the specific risks and challenges posed by different types of AI systems.

In conclusion, while the Executive Order on AI sets forth important principles, its broad and vague guidelines may not be sufficient to effectively regulate the complex and rapidly evolving field of AI. The potential for interpretation and enforcement challenges could hinder the United States' ability to lead in AI innovation. As AI continues to advance globally, the U.S. must find a way to balance the need for safety and ethics with the imperative to support and drive technological progress. The bottom line is that AI will continue to move rapidly across the globe, and any attempt to slow it down through broad executive actions may have little impact on its progress. The key will be in crafting regulations that are as agile and adaptive as the technologies they seek to govern.

Chapter 14: Sam Altman - A Proposal for a Global AI Regulatory Body

Creating an AI Regulatory Body Equivalent to the International Atomic Energy Agency (IAEA)

In an interview with Bill Gates, Sam Altman, co-founder of OpenAI, proposed the creation of a global regulatory body similar to the International Atomic Energy Agency (IAEA) for AI oversight. This body would monitor large-scale AI infrastructures, much like nuclear inspectors review nuclear installations, ensuring they adhere to global standards and do not pose security or ethical risks. Altman's suggestion reflects concerns about AI's potential for destructive use if unchecked and unregulated, akin to nuclear technology in its capacity to impact geopolitical balance and global safety.

The creation of such a regulatory body would involve setting international standards for AI development and use, ensuring compliance, and enforcing ethical AI practices globally. This body would also address emerging challenges posed by AI technologies such as Deepfakes, copyright infringement, disinformation, and AI hallucination. These issues present real risks to privacy, security, and truth in the digital age, necessitating a regulatory framework capable of managing these risks effectively.

The development and governance of AI present multifaceted challenges that require coordinated efforts across national and international levels. The legislative efforts like the EU's AI Act and the US Executive Order on AI represent significant steps toward responsible AI development. However, the complexities of AI's impact across different sectors and its inherent privacy concerns necessitate ongoing adaptation of these regulatory frameworks.

Sam Altman's proposal for a global AI regulatory body is a proactive step towards international cooperation and standardization in AI governance. As AI continues to advance and integrate more deeply into various aspects of society and industry, the need for robust, flexible, and forward-thinking policies becomes increasingly crucial. Through concerted efforts in policymaking, legal frameworks, ethical considerations, and international cooperation, we can navigate the complexities of the AI era, ensuring that AI serves the greater good of humanity.

Chapter 15: Developing Ethical Frameworks for AI Deployment

Developing ethical frameworks and guidelines for AI deployment is crucial for virtually every business. These frameworks should guide decision-making in the deployment of the rapid proliferation of AI technologies, particularly those with a direct impact on employment. They should address questions of fairness, equity, societal welfare, and moral responsibility. They should also be aligned with all applicable regulatory requirements and guidelines.

Frameworks and Guidelines for Ethical AI Development and Deployment

The development and deployment of AI bring forth significant benefits but also pose unique ethical challenges. To ensure that AI technologies are used responsibly and for the betterment of stakeholders, employees and even society, it is imperative to establish comprehensive ethical frameworks and guidelines. These frameworks should address key areas of concern, including fairness, accountability, transparency, and societal impact. Below is an overview of the essential components of such frameworks and guidelines:

1. Principles of Ethical AI

Fairness and Non-Discrimination:
AI systems should be designed and operated to treat all users fairly, without embedding or perpetuating biases based on race, gender, ethnicity, disability, or any other discriminatory factors.

Transparency and Explainability:
AI systems must be transparent in their operations, and decisions made by AI systems and platforms should be explainable to end-users and stakeholders with clearly defined logic.

Privacy and Data Governance:
AI should respect the privacy of individuals and use data in ways that are consented to, secure, and compliant with regulations like GDPR.

Accountability and Responsibility:
There should be clear accountability for AI systems' decisions and actions, including mechanisms for redress and rectification of adverse impacts.

Safety and Security:
AI systems should be secure against malicious use and should be designed to operate safely under all conditions.

Human-Centric Values:
AI should enhance human capabilities and not diminish the value of human skills and perspectives.

Stakeholder Engagement and Public Participation
When establishing ethical frameworks and guidelines for the development and deployment of AI individuals, organizations and institutions need to engage a diverse range of stakeholders and encourage widespread participation to understand societal expectations and concerns.

Continuous Monitoring and Assessment

AI systems should incorporate continuous monitoring to ensure they adhere to ethical standards and societal values. Regular assessments of the impact of AI systems on users and society should be conducted and adjustments should be implemented as necessary.

2. Regulatory Compliance and Legal Frameworks

Navigating the intersection of AI with existing legal frameworks is crucial. AI systems must comply with established laws and regulations, such as data privacy laws like GDPR. However, the unique nature of AI poses new challenges that current legal frameworks may not adequately address. Therefore, there's a pressing need to advocate for the development of new legal structures tailored to the intricacies of AI.

These frameworks should focus on ensuring that AI's advancements are aligned with public interests, protecting individuals from potential abuses or harms caused by AI technologies. They should also provide clarity to businesses and developers on AI deployment's legal boundaries.

This approach ensures that AI is not just technologically advanced but also legally sound and socially responsible.

3. AI Ethics Review Boards

The establishment of independent AI Ethics Review Boards is pivotal. These boards, comprising ethicists, legal experts, technologists, and representatives from affected communities, should have the mandate to review AI projects and initiatives critically. Their role would be to ensure that AI applications adhere to ethical standards, are socially responsible, and consider the potential impacts on diverse groups. Such boards would act as a checkpoint, providing oversight and guidance on ethical considerations and mitigating the risks associated with AI deployment.

By incorporating a broad spectrum of perspectives, these boards can foster trust in AI systems among the public and ensure that AI advancements align with societal values and norms.

4. Research and Development Ethics

Ethical considerations must be ingrained in the research and development phase of AI. Promoting ethical research practices involves ensuring transparency, accountability, and inclusivity in AI development processes. It also requires fostering interdisciplinary research collaborations that focus on the ethical, social, and legal aspects of AI. Such collaborations can yield insights into mitigating potential harms and enhancing the societal benefits of AI technologies. Ethical research in AI not only informs better technology design but also helps in understanding the broader implications of AI on society. Encouraging responsible research practices among AI developers and institutions will contribute to the development of AI technologies that are not only innovative but also ethically sound and socially beneficial.

5. Education and Awareness

Educating AI developers, users, and the broader public about the ethical dimensions of AI is essential. Awareness and understanding of AI ethics should be fostered through dedicated training programs and educational resources. This involves integrating ethical considerations into the curriculum for AI and technology-related courses and conducting workshops and seminars for practitioners in the field. Public education campaigns can also play a significant role in demystifying AI and highlighting its ethical implications.

By promoting an understanding of ethical AI deployment among all stakeholders, from developers to end-users, we can foster a more informed and conscientious approach to AI utilization. This education should not only focus on the technical aspects but also the social and ethical ramifications of AI, ensuring that individuals are equipped to make informed decisions about AI use and its impact on society.

6. Global Cooperation and Standards

Global cooperation is paramount in establishing and harmonizing international standards for AI ethics. Participating in global discussions on AI ethics is essential for developing a unified approach to AI regulation and deployment. Collaborating with international bodies and organizations facilitates the sharing of best practices and insights, fostering a global community dedicated to responsible AI development. This cooperation should aim to create consistent standards that can be adopted worldwide, ensuring that AI's benefits are globally accessible while mitigating the risks associated with its deployment. Such international collaboration also helps in addressing cross-border challenges posed by AI, such as privacy concerns and data governance, ensuring a comprehensive and cohesive approach to AI ethics on a global scale.

Conclusion

Developing ethical frameworks and guidelines for AI deployment is an ongoing, dynamic process that requires collaboration across various sectors and disciplines. By adhering to these principles and guidelines, AI's potential can be harnessed in a manner that respects human dignity, promotes societal well-being, and ensures a sustainable and equitable future. The commitment to ethical AI deployment fosters an environment where technology serves humanity's best interests, paving the way for advancements that are not only technologically sound but also ethically responsible and socially beneficial. This commitment to ethical AI is not just a moral imperative; it is essential for ensuring the trust and acceptance of AI technologies in society, ultimately leading to a future where AI and humans coexist in harmony, each augmenting the other's capabilities and potential.

Chapter 16: Global AI Wars: The Ethical Dilemma of Controlling AI Technology in the U.S.-China Tech Tug-of-War

In the modern era, the race for technological supremacy, particularly in the realm of AI, has become a new battleground for global superpowers. The "Global AI Wars" not only encompass technological advancements but also raise profound ethical questions about controlling and limiting AI capabilities across nations. This tussle is most evident in the escalating tech war between the U.S. and China, revolving around chips and raw materials necessary for AI, and the strategic importance of Taiwan Semiconductor Manufacturing Company (TSMC) in the global AI landscape.

The U.S.-China Tech War: A Battle for AI Supremacy

The ongoing tech war between the U.S. and China, represents a critical shift in global technological dynamics. The U.S. government, under the Biden administration, has implemented stringent policies to restrict the export of advanced microchips and semiconductor technologies to China. These policies aim to limit China's capacity to enhance its AI technology, especially in applications that could have military uses.

One of the pivotal moments in this tech war was the U.S. export controls enacted on October 7, 2022. This policy marked a significant change from previous approaches, targeting not just specific end-users or military uses but imposing restrictions on a geographic basis for China as a whole. The aim was to actively degrade the peak technological capability of China's semiconductor industry and prevent it from reaching certain advanced performance thresholds in semiconductor technology (CSIS.org).

The new rules have targeted chips that power high-end AI systems and the semiconductor equipment machinery aiding domestic production of leading-edge chips in China. Despite the attempt to curb China's AI computing capability, loopholes remain. For example, the leniency on lagging-edge chips and the ability of Chinese firms to access semiconductor manufacturing equipment, even for manufacturing lagging-edge chips, poses challenges to the effectiveness of these restrictions (The Diplomat).

China's response to these measures has been multifaceted. Initially, it was relatively muted, but recent developments suggest a shift in strategy. China appears to be focusing on developing homegrown capabilities in the AI industry to reduce reliance on American technology. This includes exploring alternative AI techniques, investing in memory computing, analog technology, and neuromorphic computing. Additionally, breakthroughs like Huawei's development of 7 nm technology indicate a move towards self-sufficiency in chip manufacturing (The Diplomat).

Impact on AI Development and Ethical Considerations

This AI Tech-War has far-reaching implications for AI development globally. On the one hand, the actions taken by both the U.S and China are seen as measures to protect national interests and security. On the other hand, they raise ethical concerns about the equitable growth of AI technology. Restricting access to critical AI components can hinder innovation and progress in countries facing limitations, potentially leading to a technology divide where AI advancements become concentrated in a few nations.

Taiwan's TSMC: A Linchpin in the Global AI Equation

Central to this tech war is TSMC, the world's most advanced chipmaker. The company's pivotal role in manufacturing chips essential for AI applications places it at the heart of geopolitical tensions, particularly those between China and Taiwan. TSMC, the world's largest contract chipmaker, plays a crucial role in the AI revolution. Its advanced semiconductor manufacturing capabilities are vital for AI applications which require high-performance, efficient chips to process and analyze vast amounts of data.

TSMC's Role in AI Development

TSMC is at the forefront of producing some of the most advanced semiconductor chips required for AI. These chips are essential for data centers, smartphones, and AI applications like machine learning and neural network processing. The company's ability to produce chips at the cutting edge – using 5-nanometer (and soon 3-nanometer) technology – is unmatched globally. This technological prowess places TSMC in a strategic position in the global supply chain of AI technology.

China-Taiwan Tensions and Global AI Chip Supply

The growing tensions between China and Taiwan over unification issues present a significant risk to the global supply of these advanced chips. China's ambitious goals for unification with Taiwan, if escalated into conflict, could disrupt TSMC's operations, given that its major manufacturing facilities are based in Taiwan. Such a disruption would have a profound impact on the global AI industry, as alternatives to TSMC's advanced chip manufacturing capabilities are limited. This scenario would significantly hamper the AI advancements of countries reliant on these chips, including the United States.

U.S. Dependency on TSMC

The U.S., despite being a leader in AI research and development, relies heavily on TSMC for the production of advanced semiconductor chips. American tech giants like Apple, Qualcomm, and Nvidia, which are at the forefront of AI technology, depend on TSMC for their chip supplies. A disruption in TSMC's operations due to the China-Taiwan tensions could lead to a bottleneck in the supply of critical components necessary for AI technologies, thereby impacting the United States' ability to maintain its pace in AI advancements.

Global Implications of a Disrupted Chip Supply

The global impact of a potential disruption in TSMC's operations extends beyond the U.S. It would affect a range of industries worldwide that are increasingly reliant on AI, from automotive to healthcare. The shortage of advanced chips would not only slow down the progress in AI research and applications but also lead to economic consequences due to the growing importance of AI in various sectors.

The Threat to Global AI Development

A disruption in TSMC's operations, whether due to political conflict or economic sanctions, could have a crippling effect on global AI development. Given the reliance of major tech companies and nations on TSMC's chips, any instability in this region could lead to a bottleneck in AI advancement worldwide. This situation underscores the fragility of the global tech ecosystem and the need for diversified and secure supply chains.

Ethical Dilemma: Balancing National Security with AI Growth

At the heart of the Global AI Wars is an ethical dilemma: How do nations balance the need for national security with the equitable development of AI technology? The restrictions imposed by the U.S. on China, while serving security interests, also bring up questions about the ethical implications of hindering a country's AI capabilities. This strategy could lead to an AI arms race, where countries invest heavily in AI for defense and surveillance, potentially overlooking the technology's benefits in other sectors like healthcare, environmental sustainability, and education.

The Role of International Collaboration and AI Regulations

The solution to this complex issue might lie in international collaboration and the development of global regulations for AI development and usage. Such regulations could provide a framework for the responsible growth of AI, ensuring that advancements in this field are used for the greater good rather than geopolitical dominance. This approach would require a concerted effort from nations worldwide to establish standards and guidelines that promote ethical AI development while respecting individual countries' sovereignty and security concerns.

Conclusion

The "Global AI Wars" highlight the intricate interplay of technology, geopolitics, and ethics in the modern world. As nations grapple with the challenges of AI development and its implications for global power dynamics, the need for a balanced and ethical approach becomes increasingly apparent. The future of AI should be shaped not just by the ambitions of individual nations but by a collective commitment to harnessing this transformative technology for the benefit of all humanity.

Chapter 17: What Next - Establishment of The Council on AI Ethics

In response to the growing influence of Artificial Intelligence (AI) across various sectors and its profound ethical implications, a new body, the *"Council on AI Ethics,"* is currently being established. Mirroring the framework of UNESCO's AI for the Planet organization (www.aifortheplanet.org), this council is designed to be a pivotal force in guiding ethical AI development and implementation. Chaired by Brendan Reilly, Chief AI Officer at AIworkforce.org, a member of the Advisory Board for the United Nations **AI for the Planet** organization (www.aifortheplanet.org), and author of this book. The *Council on AI Ethics* aims to serve as a central hub for addressing the myriad ethical issues posed by the rapid expansion and adoption of AI technologies.

Overview of the Council on AI Ethics

The primary objective of the Council will be to foster an environment where AI is developed and utilized in ways that respect human rights, promote societal welfare, and uphold ethical standards. It aims to bridge the gap between technological advancements and ethical considerations, ensuring AI's benefits are maximized while its risks are minimized.

Structure and Membership:

The Council will comprise a diverse group of experts, including AI technologists, ethicists, legal professionals, and representatives from various industries impacted by AI. This multidisciplinary composition ensures a comprehensive approach to AI ethics, encompassing a wide range of perspectives and expertise.

Functions and Responsibilities:

1. **Guideline Development:**
   The Council will focus on developing ethical guidelines for AI, which serve as a framework for companies and organizations in their AI endeavors.

2. **Policy Recommendations:**
   It will advise policymakers on AI-related issues, ensuring that laws and regulations align with ethical standards.

3. **Awareness and Education:**
   The Council will play a key role in educating the public about AI ethics, promoting an understanding of both the opportunities and challenges posed by AI.

4. **Stakeholder Collaboration:**
   It will encourage collaboration between various stakeholders, including governments, private sectors, academia, and civil society, fostering a unified approach to ethical AI.

Strategic Initiatives:

Research and Innovation:
The Council will support research on ethical AI, encouraging innovation that aligns with ethical principles.

Global Standards: It will work towards establishing global ethical standards for AI, facilitating international cooperation and consensus.

Ethical Audits: The Council promotes the implementation of ethical audits for AI systems, ensuring compliance with established guidelines.

Challenges and Opportunities:

The Council acknowledges the challenges in balancing AI innovation with ethical considerations. It is committed to addressing these challenges, recognizing the opportunity to set a global precedent in ethical AI governance.

Conclusion

The establishment of the Council on AI Ethics represents a significant step towards responsible AI development and use. Under the leadership of Brendan Reilly and with the collective expertise of its members, the Council is poised to make a meaningful impact in the realm of AI ethics. Its initiatives and guidelines will not only influence current AI practices but also shape the future of AI development, ensuring it advances in a manner that respects ethical values and promotes the greater good of society.

Chapter 18: The Final Word

As we reach the final pages of this exploration into the world of Artificial Intelligence (AI), it is clear that we stand at a pivotal crossroads. AI technologies present a panorama of tremendous opportunities, yet they also carry risks potent enough to reshape the very fabric of human existence. These risks, if left unchecked, have the potential to trigger an existential crisis for workers, industries, communities, and the broader societal framework.

The Existential Risk to Human Workers

AI's capacity to displace jobs, a theme recurrent throughout this book, casts a long shadow over the future of work. From truck drivers facing the advent of autonomous vehicles to accountants and lawyers whose roles are increasingly automated, the potential for widespread unemployment and underemployment is palpable. This seismic shift in the labor market calls for a paradigm change in how we view employment, skill development, and economic sustainability.

The Imperative for Oversight and Regulatory Controls

The unchecked progression of AI could lead to scenarios where its ability to displace jobs drastically outpaces humanity's capacity to create new ones.

This imbalance necessitates stringent oversight and regulatory controls. Governments, international bodies, and industry leaders must collaborate to establish frameworks that ensure AI's development is balanced, ethical, and aligned with human welfare.

The Threats Beyond Job Displacement

The scope of AI's impact extends beyond the job market. Technologies like deepfake and AI-enhanced mass surveillance represent profound threats to privacy, security, and the very essence of truth and trust in our societies. The potential for misuse in spreading misinformation, manipulating public opinion, and infringing upon individual rights is a stark reminder of the darker facets of AI.

The Pioneering Stage of the AI Revolution

We find ourselves in the nascent stages of the AI revolution – a revolution that, if not guided wisely, could evolve into societal upheaval or even conflict. The decisions we make today, the policies we implement, and the ethical standards we set will determine whether this revolution will be a catalyst for unprecedented growth and innovation or a harbinger of disruption and discord.

The Ethical Frontier: Balancing Innovation and Humanity

At the heart of navigating AI's impact lies the ethical frontier – the delicate balance between harnessing AI's transformative power and preserving the fundamental values of humanity. As AI reshapes industries and redefines roles, it also tests our moral compass, challenging us to rethink the principles that govern technology and society.

The Role of Education and Lifelong Learning

A key strategy in adapting to AI's influence is education. Educational systems must evolve to provide not only technical skills in AI and related fields but also foster critical thinking, creativity, and ethical understanding. Lifelong learning emerges as a necessity, not a luxury, equipping individuals to navigate a constantly changing job landscape.

The Necessity for Global Dialogue and Collaboration

Addressing the challenges and harnessing the opportunities of AI requires a global dialogue and collaborative efforts. No single entity or nation can tackle the complexities of AI in isolation. International standards, shared ethical guidelines, and cooperative research and development efforts are crucial in creating a unified approach to AI governance.

The Future of AI: A Balanced Trajectory

As we envisage the future of AI, it is essential to strive for a balanced trajectory where technological advancement and human welfare are not seen as mutually exclusive. AI must be developed and deployed in ways that augment human capabilities, enrich lives, and foster societal progress.

Conclusion: A Call to Responsible Action

In closing, "Navigating the Ethical Frontier: The Impact of AI on Society and Work" serves as both a mirror and a beacon. It reflects the complexities, challenges, and potentials of AI, urging us to deliberate, discuss, and take decisive action. As we stand at this juncture in the journey of AI, the choices we make, the policies we enact, and the ethical standards we uphold will shape not only the future of AI but the future of humanity itself.

The AI revolution offers a path to a brighter, more efficient, and more connected world. However, this path is fraught with ethical quandaries and societal risks. It is up to us – technologists, policymakers, ethicists, and society at large – to ensure that this revolution evolves harmoniously, not disruptively. The journey ahead is complex, but with careful navigation, informed decision-making, and a commitment to ethical integrity, we can steer the AI revolution towards a future that benefits all of humanity.

ABOUT THE AUTHOR

As an accomplished Big Data, AI, Clean Energy, and Climate Risk technology entrepreneur and philanthropist, the author Brendan Reilly's career has spanned over three decades encompassing various leadership positions around the world.

Presently, Brendan serves as the Founder and Chief AI Officer at AIworkforce.org. He serves as the Chairman at the Climate Risk Research Foundation, a 501(c)(3) entity dedicated to climate-related research, he is the Head of AI and Corporate Development at the Linux Foundation's OS-Climate and serves as an Advisory Board Member at the United Nations - AI For The Planet.

Previously, Mr. Reilly served as the Co-founder and CTO at Riskthinking.AI, where he developed an innovative AI-driven Climate Risk Scenario Generation Platform and Climate Risk Data Exchange before helping orchestrate a large strategic alliance and Series A investment with Bloomberg L.P.

As the current Chairman of the Climate Risk Research Foundation, Brendan leads an organization focused on conducting data-driven research to confront global climate challenges in the global south.
Brendan is a co-founder of 9H Energy and 9H Research Foundation, where he spearheaded the development of a Solar Energy Research Facility in collaboration with the University of Wyoming School of Engineering and continues to support the long-term goal of building a Utility-Scale Solar Generation and Energy Storage Facility in Southeast Wyoming.

In his early career, Brendan co-founded Storage Area Networks Inc. which he helped grow to a NASDAQ-listed company and $100M in revenue prior to selling the company in 2003. Brendan was the seed investor or co-founder in six high-tech start-ups, two of which exceeded $100 million in revenue before being divested, one went public, two were sold to publicly traded companies, and three were strategically divested in private transactions.

Brendan's career is distinguished by leading AI and data-driven projects within the U.S Department of Defense, the Intelligence Community, and numerous Fortune 500 companies. Holding a top-secret security clearance for many years, Brendan directed critical data and AI driven projects at the FBI, U.S Army, DLA, DISA, DTRA, Defense Health Agency, U.S Marine Corps, and at corporations including Goldman Sachs, Microsoft, S&P, Marriott Corp, NYSE, Bank of New York Mellon, Ping An Bank, China Light & Power, and dozens of other large multinationals corporations. Brendan has served as a Director for businesses in the U.S, England, Ireland, Canada, Hong Kong, China and the United Arab Emirates.

Brendan is an alumnus of Providence College and Harvard Business School and a devoted father of five.

CITATIONS & REFERENCES

1. https://www.mckinsey.com/featured-insights/future-of-work/jobs-lost-jobs-gained-what-the-future-of-work-will-mean-for-jobs-skills-and-wages

2. https://www.mckinsey.com/mgi/our-research/generative-ai-and-the-future-of-work-in-america

3. https://www.thecrimson.com/article/2023/10/13/jagged-edge-ai-bcg/

4. https://www.mckinsey.com/industries/metals-and-mining/our-insights/succeeding-in-the-ai-supply-chain-revolution

5. https://www.forbes.com/sites/louiscolumbus/2017/06/22/artificial-intelligence-will-enable-38-profit-gains-by-2035/?sh=299e92c61969

6. https://www.forbes.com/sites/kalinabryant/2023/05/31/how-ai-will-impact-the-next-generation-workforce/?sh=5941a8fb6fae

7. https://www.vox.com/2016/8/3/12342764/autonomous-trucks-employment

8. https://www.indeed.com/career/long-haul-driver/salaries

9. https://www.statista.com/statistics/317587/number-of-accountants-and-auditors-employed-us/

10. https://www.statista.com/statistics/740222/number-of-lawyers-us/

11. https://www.ncarb.org/press/2020-number-of-us-architects-continues-upward-trend

12. https://datausa.io/profile/soc/writers-authors

13. https://open.spotify.com/episode/2TeIwqNMI0gv8NCRyEebJR?si=3wKCzaC0SpSOb83_4sGa_Q

14. https://www.bls.gov/oes/current/oes151252.htm.

15. https://www.bls.gov/ooh/Office-and-Administrative-Support/Customer-service-representatives.htm

16. https://www.bls.gov/oes/current/oes132052.htm

17. https://pwc.blogs.com/press_room/2017/03/up-to-30-of-existing-uk-jobs-could-be-impacted-by-automation-by-early-2030s-but-this-should-be-offse.html

18. https://www.gsam.com/content/gsam/global/en/market-insights/gsam-insights/perspectives/2023/artificial-intelligence-future.html#:~:text=We%20believe%20that%20approximately%20two,of%20jobs%20could%20be%20displaced.

19. https://www.uipath.com/blog/ai/ai-tools-will-allow-humans-to-work-creatively#:~:text=A%20study%20by%20%E2%80%9Cresearchers%20from,perspective%20towards%20work%20and%20automation.

20. https://fred.stlouisfed.org/series/BA06RC1A027NBEA

21. https://www.bls.gov/emp/graphics/total-employment.htm

22. https://www.europarl.europa.eu/news/en/press-room/20231206IPR15699/artificial-intelligence-act-deal-on-comprehensive-rules-for-trustworthy-ai

Send Comments, Though or Suggestions to:
breilly@aiworkforce.org

AIworkforce.org

www.ingramcontent.com/pod-product-compliance
Lightning Source LLC
Chambersburg PA
CBHW071057290526
45795CB00004B/1534